The British Horse Society

Career Pathways

Ride Safe

A modern approach to riding safely in all environments

Supporting you through every stage

Acknowledgements

We would like to thank all those who have been involved in the development and production of Ride Safe including Berkshire Riding Centre, Jon Stroud Media, Tara Taylor Photography and Lottie-Elizabeth Photography.

Waymarker images kindly supplied by Metrosigns2000.co.uk
Low-flying aircraft image courtesy of MoD (page 78)
The Official Highway Code Crown Copyright.

First published in the UK in 2017 by Kenilworth Press,
an imprint of Quiller Publishing Ltd

Revised edition 2020

British Library Cataloguing-in-Publication Data
A catalogue record for this book is available from the British Library

ISBN 978 1 910016 26 8

Printed in the UK

Kenilworth Press

An imprint of Quiller Publishing Ltd
Wykey House, Wykey, Shrewsbury SY4 1JA
Tel: 01939 261616
E-mail: info@quillerbooks.com
Website: www.kenilworthpress.co.uk

Contents

Welcome to Ride Safe

'Riding or driving horses is a wonderful way to enjoy the countryside and your local area outside of the arena, or somewhere new.

Ride Safe provides a foundation for any rider to be safe and knowledgeable when riding in all environments including on and off the road, and warming up at competitions.

Your *Ride Safe* guide provides a comprehensive understanding with practical examples, tips and guidance ideal for all riders from occasional riders to elite equestrians.

While providing a friendly and supportive environment to learn in, the Ride Safe Award works to keep you and your horse safe and could even save lives.'

The British Horse Society

Most riders will at some point ride out of the arena and enjoy hacking on and off roads, beaches and forests. As we all know, there are risks associated but these can be reduced by having knowledge of riding out on the road and interacting with other countryside users.

There are, however, some simple things that you can do and be aware of to help ensure the safety of your horse, yourself and others when riding on the road, equestrian route or in an arena.

Chapter 1

Before I Leave the Yard

Can I lead a horse safely?

Can I mount and dismount safely?

Can I perform an emergency dismount,
lead and remount?

Is my horse up to date with the farrier?

Is my horse's tack in good condition
and fitted correctly?

What about me?

Can I lead a horse safely?

Most of us will lead our horses on a daily basis around the yard or field without really thinking anything of it. But when leading a horse on and off the road there are a few extra things to remember to help keep you both safe. It is strongly recommended that the horse wears a bridle to improve your control and you should position yourself between the horse and the traffic and other route users. This means the horse will be on your left on the road. The reins should be taken over the horse's head to lead with, unless the horse is wearing a running martingale. Otherwise the martingale can become tangled with the reins and affect your control. It is best to hold both reins in the left hand.

If you are riding and leading, the led horse needs to be wearing a bridle, with the reins passed through the bit rings to the rider's left hand, so the unridden horse is on the inside and the ridden horse is between the led horse and the traffic or other route users (e.g. cyclists).

Can I mount and dismount safely?

There may be times where you will be required to get on and off, for example when opening or closing a gate, leading your horse over a bridge with low sides or picking a stone out of your horse's hoof. Remember that there may not be a raised platform available to help you get on and off. If you rely on this to mount, it is advisable to check your planned route beforehand. If there are places where riders would regularly require the use of a mounting block and they are not available, like at a bridge or gate, you can report this to your local council, as they may be able to help. This also applies to gates on equestrian routes that cannot be opened from horseback.

To find further guidance and help, please visit bhs.org.uk

Can I perform an emergency dismount, lead and remount?

We advise that you only dismount while out hacking if it is really necessary. It is usually safer for you and your horse if you remain mounted. However, you may have occasion to perform an emergency dismount. It is important to be able to dismount, lead and remount on both sides proficiently so that you are safe and in control of your horse at all times.

Please use the steps below as guidance to be able to perform an emergency dismount, lead and remount.

Dismount

- Look behind you to ensure no cars or other route users (e.g. cyclists or walkers) are approaching and find a safe place to dismount, if possible off the road. Your horse should be positioned with his hindquarters slightly in.

- Look again before taking both feet out of the stirrups. Cross your right stirrup over first in front of the saddle (on the horse's shoulder). If possible, dismount away from traffic on the left; make sure you remember to transfer your whip into the left hand; or the side you are dismounting from.

- Place the stirrups over the seat of the saddle, so they are not hitting the side of the horse.

- Check all around for traffic – quickly but carefully put yourself between your horse and the traffic and take the reins over your horse's head to lead him, unless he is wearing a running martingale.

Lead

- Look behind you, signal if necessary before you move off, and, if clear, with the reins in both hands and whip in the right hand, walk on.

- Keep looking around while leading.

- Find a safe place to remount.

Remount

- Put the reins back over your horse's head and check the girth.

- Check it is safe before you move back round to the nearside.

- If all appears safe, take down the nearside stirrup and place the whip in your left hand.

- Remount and transfer the whip back into your right hand. Put the other stirrup down once mounted. Make sure you look all around you before moving off. A signal may be required.

> **Near and off side explained**
>
> The nearside of a horse is the horse's left side and the off side is the horse's right side.

We would recommend you mount and dismount from the nearside in the UK and Republic of Ireland. It is good practice to be able to mount and dismount from both sides, and where possible use mounting blocks or raised ground to reduce the strain on your horse's back.

Is my horse up to date with the farrier?

Most horses require a visit from the farrier approximately every four to six weeks; but it is important to check their feet between visits to ensure their hooves or shoes don't require attention. This will reduce the danger of your horse slipping or tripping when out hacking, particularly on uneven ground, which is common on equestrian routes.

Is my horse's tack in good condition and fitted correctly?

This is important for all riding, not just hacking. It is extremely important to check your tack before you ride as you may not be very close to home should a problem arise.

- It is important to get your saddle checked regularly by a professional at least twice a year.

- Tack should be flexible and supple so it is comfortable for the horse and won't cause sores.

- The stitching, buckles and leather should be in good order to prevent breakages.

- Check that the stirrup bars on the saddle are in the down position and that the stirrup irons are the right size for your feet. There should be a minimum of 6mm (one finger's width) each side of your foot in the stirrup.

What about me?

Is your hat up to the latest safety standard and are your boots and clothing safe?

- Your hat is essential, and should be correctly fitted, with all straps properly adjusted with your chinstrap fastened and secured.

- The safety standard which applies to your hat will appear on the inside of the helmet. We would always recommend your helmet meets the current safety standard and relevant quality assurance mark.

For the latest hat standards please visit bhs.org.uk

- Your footwear should have a hard sole and a small heel (so your feet do not slip through the irons), and ideally cover your calf so that the stirrup leather does not pinch. Soft footwear is not advised as it won't have the correct grip and offers little protection to your toes.

- Where possible, wear a long-sleeved top to give your arms some protection. It's easy to be scratched on narrow lanes or equestrian routes.

- We recommend gloves to improve your grip on the reins, especially in the wet. If you usually ride with a whip, remember to take it with you.

Are you wearing high visibility clothing?

High visibility clothing isn't everyone's favourite, but it really is some of the most important equipment that you and your horse will own. By choosing to wear conspicuous clothing you are enabling drivers, motorcyclists, cyclists and walkers to see you significantly earlier, giving traffic time to slow down and pass you carefully and safely. It really can make the difference between coming home safe and sound and having an incident on the road. Conspicuous clothing will also make it easier for people to find you and come to your aid should you have the misfortune to have a fall or accident.

There are many different kinds of high visibility kit for you and your horse, and a selection of colours that can either be reflective or fluorescent (or both). Fluorescent materials show up in the daylight but have no special qualities in the dark. Reflective materials will reflect a light source in either the day or night, so are essential during fading daylight hours and at night.

As a minimum, we recommend a high visibility vest for yourself and you should consider an exercise sheet and high visibility boots or wraps for your horse. High visibility boots/wraps might not be the most obvious piece of essential equipment but they have been found to be seen easily by drivers as they sit at eye level. The constant movement of the horse's legs help to catch the driver's eye and, should you have an incident and come off your horse, it helps your horse to be seen.

Please refer to the *Highway Code* section of this guide, in particular to find out what items you and your horse are required to wear.

The picture on the right shows the importance of wearing high visibility clothing on and off road. We do not recommend riding in the dark, however should you find yourself in failing light or a shaded area you can see the importance in wearing high visibility clothing. It enables you and your horse to stand out against the background. It also allows drivers, cyclists and walkers to see you and your horse sooner, which means they have more time to slow down and pass you safely.

Don't be a dark horse – Hi Viz – bhs.org.uk/Advice-for-Motorists

Standards

Most high visibility clothing now reaches BSI approved standards. This standard can be found on the BHS website bhs.org.uk/advice-for-motorists.

Am I safe and secure in walk, trot and canter and could I deal confidently with my horse if he reacts to a potential hazard?

We recommend that you are able to walk, trot and preferably canter securely with your horse before you ride out on the road or in an open space. There are many potential hazards that can startle horses and cause them to react unexpectedly. If you have a secure seat you will be better prepared to cope with an unexpected situation that might spook your horse, like a flapping piece of rubbish in a hedgerow.

Do I have insurance?

Some riders are not aware of their insurance needs. Should your horse cause damage to another person or property, you may be liable to pay considerable costs. All riders and horse owners are strongly advised to hold public liability insurance, which protects you in cases like this, with your insurer covering some, or all, of the cost of any damages. If you are a BHS Gold member you have public liability insurance within your membership, for all horses you ride or own. Terms, conditions and territorial limits apply.

BHS Membership

For more questions regarding the comprehensive insurance available through BHS membership, please contact the BHS membership department on 02476 840506.

In a group of ridden horses, collecting ring or whilst out riding, you may see horses with a coloured ribbon in their tail. This is a universally recognised, straightforward way of alerting other riders and route users to a particular horse. The two most common ribbon colours you will see are red and green.

- **Red** means this horse may kick if another horse gets too close. It is your responsibility to keep your horse at a safe distance, so plan where you are going to avoid getting too close to other route users.

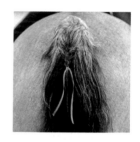

- **Green** means this is a young or inexperienced horse. These horses may be spooky, react unexpectedly or the rider may not be able to turn or stop quickly. If your horse needs this ribbon in his tail, you should be escorted out on the road by a more experienced horse and rider.

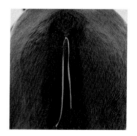

- Consider using ribbons when riding on the road. Drivers are being made aware of the relevance of these ribbons.

Summary

- When leading a horse on and off the road the horse should wear a bridle and you should always walk between the horse and the traffic to give you better control of your horse.

- Always ensure your tack is in good condition before setting off with the stirrup bars in the down position.

- Your hat is essential. You need to ensure it is fitted correctly and is up to date with the latest hat standards.

- High visibility clothing is essential to wear when out and about. It is important to know the difference between fluorescent and reflective clothing.

- Fluorescent materials show up in the daylight but have no special qualities in the dark. We do not recommend riding on the road in the dark.

- Reflective materials will reflect a light source in either the day or night, so are essential on dull days.

- Public liability is the minimum insurance a rider should have: the BHS Gold membership can offer this.

TRAINING TIPS

1. Practise leading your horse in a bridle as you would on the road (i.e. with yourself between the horse and traffic).

2. Practise mounting and dismounting without someone holding the horse, from either side of the horse. This will help should you need to perform an emergency dismount.

3. Ensure your horse is fit, healthy and prepared to ride out. Speak to your farrier to see what signs to look out for when checking his shoes daily.

Chapter 2

Setting Off

What should I be aware of when
preparing to ride out?

Have I told someone where I am going?

Do I know how to ride out alone,
in pairs and in a group?

What should I do in the event
of an incident?

What should I be aware of when preparing to ride out?

At certain times of the day traffic may be busier than usual and you may want to avoid taking your horse out for a ride. You will soon get to know how much the roads around your stables are affected by rush-hour traffic, such as school opening and closure times. At such times the volume of traffic may increase and some vehicles may be travelling quicker than usual as the drivers are eager to get to their destination, and may be less likely to slow down for you.

The time of year can also have an impact on what traffic you will see on the roads – for example large haulage vehicles, heavy farm machinery – or you may meet your local hunt and followers. During late summer and early autumn you may see more tractors and large trailers on the road as farmers collect in their harvest before winter arrives. Farmers typically work long hours so it is not particularly easy to avoid them. If your horse is nervous of tractors and trailers, ride into a driveway and let the tractor pass you, or ask the driver to stop and turn their engine off and let you pass slowly.

The hunting season falls throughout autumn and winter, with most hunts operating on specific weekdays and Saturdays. They will usually have a large number of horses and foot-followers, which may excite your horse should you meet them. This is something to be aware of as you plan your rides.

Riding in a group

If you are riding out in a group we recommend the lead and last rider (or the outside rider if riding in a pair) not only wear conspicuous equipment but also have a light showing white to the front and red to the rear. Your horse should always be wearing appropriate fluorescent and reflective equipment too – this helps other road users see you sooner.

Surface conditions

There are certain road conditions that can be a danger to you and your horse, and you can come across these all year round:

● Worn, shiny patches on the road.

- Uneven road surface, especially on a bend or corner.

- Potholes and drain covers.

- Loose grit and wet leaves.

- Fencing, barbed wire and electric fencing.

- Mud, flooding and subsidence.

All of the above can be slippery or may cause your horse to trip or stumble. To avoid an accident or injury ride around them and adjust your speed. You can also ask your farrier for anti-slip nails and shoes that provide your horse with more grip.

Weather

Snow and ice can make the routes exceptionally slippery and dangerous and we recommend that you don't ride at all in dark and icy/snowy conditions. However, should it be completely unavoidable to ride on the road in snow and ice, keep your horse at a walk and do not hurry him or have too tight a rein contact. Try to ride or lead as near to the kerb, verge or edge of the road as is safely possible, as the accumulation of grit here will give your horse more grip. If your horse does slip or fall, do not panic, stay calm and allow your horse to regain his footing, remembering to check for injury afterwards.

Windy weather is another common challenge, which can make it harder for you to listen out for traffic and other road users. It may also make a horse tense and spookier than usual. Be extra vigilant for things like rubbish, gates and haylage bale wrap flapping around. During winter months there is, of course, less daylight and more bad weather to take into consideration. You may find that low sun might also be a challenge in the winter months as this will make visibility even harder for other route users. Plan carefully so that you don't find yourself riding home in dusk or darkness. However, dull or misty days are hard to avoid in the winter, so dress appropriately by wearing high visibility clothing for both you and your horse, making sure you are wearing both fluorescent clothing on and off the road and reflective equipment.

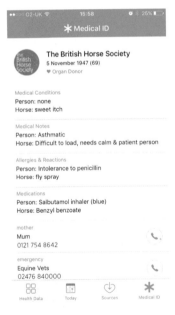

Have I told someone where I am going?

It is good practice to let someone else know where you plan to go, and roughly how long the hack should take you, so they might raise the alarm if you fail to return within a reasonable time. Taking a fully charged mobile phone with you is a good idea; however, avoid using it while mounted. Make sure you have important phone numbers like the vet and a close friend or family member stored in the phone so they are readily available.

You should also have saved 'In Case of Emergency' (ICE) numbers and information on your phone. In the event of an accident, those first on the scene are then able to contact whoever it is you have identified as your next of kin through the ICE numbers, under 'ICE1, ICE2', etc. Important medical information may be required from this contact should paramedics or the hospital need it. On most smart phones now there is an option to fill out a personal medical ID too, which is accessible even if your phone is locked. It might also be a good idea to have bridle and saddle tags on your horse in case you get separated.

You can also download an APP 'What3words' which has been designed to help locate people easily in remote areas and is used by the emergency services.

Do I know how to ride out alone, in pairs and in a group?

Alone – If you ride out alone, try to do so on a horse that you know and are confident on. Make sure you let somebody know where you are going and when to expect you back. Fluorescent or reflective clothing for you and the horse is extremely important, as is a mobile, so you can contact someone in an emergency.

In pairs (double file) – The *Highway Code* does not require riders to travel in single file, though in the general guidance it says it may be advisable to ride in single file. The ultimate decision is up to you as the rider.

For example, if you are escorting a young or inexperienced horse or rider, they may need to be on the inside. If this is not the case it is safer to ride in single file where traffic and road conditions require you to, e.g. on narrow roads, or in heavy traffic and when riding round bends. To move between double and single file, the outside horse moves either in front or behind the horse on the inside, as appropriate. Both horses and riders should wear high visibility clothing. Be particularly careful to observe behind you before changing from single to double or double to single file and thanking traffic.

In groups – When riding out in groups make sure the group sizes are sensible, ideally not bigger than eight, for reasons of safety and practicality. When on the road in a large group, for example on a sponsored ride, try to ride in double file, leaving half a horse's length between each pair. The pairs can be divided into small groups, leaving a minimum gap of 30m between them, to allow traffic to overtake as safely as possible. In some circumstances you may find it more practical to remain as one large group. If this is the case, cross road junctions as a single controlled group that is monitored and overseen by the lead rider. The lead rider should understand their legal and insurance responsibilities before escorting riders on to the public highway. The lead and rear rider in the group should give the signals and communicate with other road users, setting a pace that is suitable for the whole group.

Young horse or novice rider

If you are riding a young, inexperienced or nervous horse try to take him out initially with another rider on a more experienced and relaxed horse. You may want to ride double file with the nervous horse on the inside so he is more sheltered from the traffic while he builds his confidence. It would be sensible to avoid peak traffic times and pick routes you believe to be quieter. This may also apply if you are riding an exceptionally fit horse that could be excitable or unpredictable.

The same applies to a young or inexperienced rider. A more experienced horse and rider accompanying them can help teach them the skills and awareness they need to ride on the road, build their confidence and assist them should they get into any difficulty. You may again want to ride in double file, with the less experienced rider on the inside, so they are more sheltered from traffic. We recommend *anyone* riding a horse wears a hat but remember that children under the age of 14 *must* wear a hat which is up to current standards and it must be fastened securely according to the *Highway Code*.

(These requirements do not apply to a child who is a follower of the Sikh religion and wearing a turban).

Where can I ride?

There are some beautiful places in which to ride and drive a carriage in the UK and Ireland. Some of us have access to long stretches of safe, well maintained routes, whilst others must rely only on beach or forestry access. Others have little or no access to such places, with many routes being fragmented, inaccessible, or with no off-road options at all. Wherever you are, you must understand where you can and cannot take your horse. By doing a little investigatory work, you may find routes you didn't even know existed and soon set off on a completely new adventure on horseback. The BHS Access & Rights of Way (ARoW) team have produced a great leaflet to get you started in finding new routes in your area. Please note that legislation on riding differs according to where you live in England, Wales, Scotland, Northern Ireland and the Republic of Ireland.

Countdown to 2026

Off-road areas are under threat for use to horse riders in England and will be lost if they are not formally recorded as a bridleway by 2026. How can you help? Visit here to find out: bhs.org.uk/2026.

The BHS national equestrian route network consists of long and short distance linear and circular routes throughout the UK and Republic of Ireland. The vast majority of these can be viewed by visiting the website: bhsaccess. org.uk/ridemaps

If you are new to the area or are trying to find some new routes in your local area, then have a look at our leaflet – 'Finding new places to ride and carriage drive' by visiting bhs.org.uk

What should I do in the event of an incident?

Accidents can happen even to the best-prepared or most experienced riders. The risk of your horse being startled or behaving out of the ordinary is increased when out hacking. Accidents naturally cause a fair amount of panic, but if you know what action to take, you can minimise the impact to yourself and your horse. Remember:

● Do not take any risks yourself that could endanger your safety or anyone else's.

- **Make the situation safe** – If you can, send someone to warn approaching traffic to slow down and to try to catch any horse that is loose.

- **Ask for help** – Make contact with the appropriate emergency services and a local vet if they are required, and call a nearby friend or family member. If you do not have a phone with you, try to flag down passing road users or knock on the door of a local house and ask politely to use their phone.

- **Reassure the casualty** – Try to keep them calm and warm. Do not remove their hat and try to avoid moving them unnecessarily.

- **First aid** – If necessary and you are trained, start to apply basic first aid to the casualty. If you are not trained then wait for the emergency services to arrive or follow instructions from the emergency call centre.

Incidents can happen at any time in any environment, and can include a road accident, incident or near miss. We encourage all those that have been involved in an incident or near miss to report it to us, so we can use this data to educate and campaign for future safety improvements. See bhs.org/reportanincident

Have you remembered your insurance? For further advice, contact our membership department on 02476 840506.

Summary

- Should you be unlucky enough to be involved in an accident, make the situation safe, ask for help, reassure the casualty and administer first aid if you are trained, until the emergency services arrive.

- Remember your safety is paramount; ensure you never put yourself in danger.

- If you are involved in an accident ensure you tell us by going onto the website bhs.org/reportanincident: this helps us try to make the roads safer.

- Ensure you always take out a fully charged mobile phone when out hacking, so you can contact someone should you need to in an emergency. It is also helpful to put in your phone emergency contact numbers and any health conditions you may have.

- If you find a blocked route whilst out hacking you can contact your local council or the BHS Access department on 02476 840515 for further advice.

TRAINING TIPS

1. If you are regularly hacking out and over the age of 16 years it might be an idea to attend a first aid course. We offer these training courses all over the UK: available courses can be found at bhs. org.uk/pathways. For Irish and Scottish dates please contact your National manager.

2. Have a look at our BHS Access leaflets or the website to see if you can find an off-road route you didn't know about.

3. Ensure you have read the legislation for riding off-road in your specific location.

Chapter 3

Sharing Routes with Other Users

Do I know how to signal to other route users?

Verges, cycle lanes, bridges and underpasses – what do I need to know?

Do I know how to signal to other route users?

Some simple road skills when riding can help make sure your experience of riding on the road is a positive one.

- **Observations** – Make sure you look all around, listen carefully for other route users and assess your surroundings before making any manoeuvre or turn on the road or equestrian route. When you look around, try to turn from your waist, enabling you to keep both hands on the reins. Always make final checks over your right shoulder immediately before carrying out a manoeuvre or moving off.

- **Positioning** – Ride in the same direction as the flow of traffic. Sometimes on narrow lanes with no verge it may be necessary to move over into a more central position but always be ready to move out of the way and be aware of changes in the road conditions and blind bends which can affect your visibility. You may need to apply more leg pressure on the right side to prevent the horse from swinging his hindquarters into the road. Take a good position at junctions so you can see traffic approaching from any direction and always look, listen and look again before manoeuvring out of a junction.

- **Signalling** – Signalling is a vital skill. It is our way of letting other route users know where we are going, if we intend to turn, or if there is a situation to be aware or cautious of. Make sure all signals or acknowledgements you give to other route users give a driver enough time to react and are clear and visible, whilst maintaining your position on the left hand side. These are the signals you should be confident using before you ride out on the road or other equestrian routes:

  - ❏ **Turning left** – Your arm must be fully extended at the height of your shoulder, with fingers and thumb close together and the palm of your hand facing forwards. Hold your signal long enough to inform other route users of your planned manoeuvre, repeating it as necessary, depending on the route conditions and behaviour of your horse.

  - ❏ **Turning right** – This can be more dangerous as you may be turning across another lane of traffic. Extend your right arm fully at the height of your shoulder with fingers and thumb closed together and the palm of your hand facing forwards. Again, hold your signal long enough to inform other route users of your planned manoeuvre, repeating it as necessary, depending on the route conditions and behaviour of your horse.

Turning Right in the Republic of Ireland

Please note that if you are riding in the Republic of Ireland, according to the Road Safety Authority, you are requested to maintain your position in the centre of the road to make a right turn. However advice from local enforcement agencies do not agree with this ruling. Always make sure you are in the safest place possible.

- ❑ **Slow down** – If you are trying to slow down traffic from behind, turn in your saddle to face the traffic coming from behind. Fully extend your right arm with the palm of your hand facing downwards and move your arm slowly upwards and downwards repeatedly.

- ❑ **Stop** – If you are trying to stop traffic from behind, turn in your saddle to face the traffic coming from behind you and use your right arm in the extended position, holding the palm of your hand towards the driver.

❑ **Thank you** – Many route users will be very considerate so it is important to thank them. You may do this verbally, with a nod of your head and a smile, or by raising your hand if it is safe to do so.

Verges, cycle lanes, bridges and underpasses – what do I need to know?

● **Grass verges** – In most places in England, Scotland and Wales riding along a verge is allowed for horse riders. Be aware of possible rubbish, bottles and drains that may be covered over by the grass and hedgerow. There may also be ditches that run alongside the verge, which your horse could slip or fall into, so remember to ride with this in mind.

It is illegal to ride on grass verges in the Republic of Ireland.

● **Cycle lanes (*England and Wales only*)** – You must not ride in a cycle lane marked by a solid white line during its times of operation. Do not ride in a cycle lane marked by a broken white line unless it is unavoidable. When planning your route you can find out any time restrictions on your route. You may want to check these out beforehand.

- **Bridges, underpasses and level crossings** – To minimise the risk of an accident, always wait for pedestrians to cross first at these crossings. In some cases restricted headroom may require you to dismount and lead your horse. At railway bridges, always check to see if there is a train approaching. If so, pull over in good time and wait for it to pass. Do not attempt to ride under a bridge until the train has passed. It will be very loud and may cause your horse to spook and become unsettled. At level crossings be alert to what the signals are telling you; they will flash when trains are approaching and it is unsafe to cross.

Summary

- Ensure any signals you give are clear and long enough for other route users to see.

- Grass verges are not always a very good place to ride: there may be rubbish or tripping hazards, so it is best to avoid them.

- In the Republic of Ireland you are required to maintain your position in the centre of the road to make a right turn. You will need to be aware that vehicles may be on both sides of you and your horse.

TRAINING TIPS

1. Practise different hand signals with friends and see if they can tell what you are asking of them when they are standing directly behind you.

2. Practise observing over your shoulder with friends and see if they can see your face clearly when you are looking behind you.

Chapter 4

Potential Hazards

Potential hazards and dangerous situations –
how should I handle them?

Potential hazards and dangerous situations – how should I handle them?

Be alert

Look around you regularly to check for changes or hazards on your route, particularly ones that may approach from behind as these are more likely to spook your horse. Listen out for approaching cars, cyclists or walkers so you can reassure your horse before they come into view. Be aware of children, families or dogs playing in gardens or close to the roadside as your horse may be able to hear but not see them, which may be frightening.

It would be a great idea to have a look at local events that might be happening. If a cycle event is on you might expect more bikes on the road along with cars and spectators. It may be worth avoiding hacking out when the event is taking place.

Bends

Approach bends in the road, and corners, at a walk as the road surface could be slippery. Be particularly aware of any traffic in front of or behind you on the approach. On left-hand bends and turns always check over your left shoulder for any pedestrians or cyclists approaching on your nearside; be sure to follow the same practice when turning right.

Traffic lights

Traffic light signals mean the same thing for horse riders as other road users: red – stop; amber – stop, and green – move off if it is safe to do so.

Be sure to observe the traffic situation carefully as you approach and be aware that some vehicles will cross the lights on amber even if you think they are going to stop. If you are turning right, some lane markings may take you into the centre of the road. This may be unsafe, as traffic will be passing you on your nearside and towards you. If traffic does not allow you to turn right safely, ride straight over the traffic lights. When safe to do so, make a U-turn across the road and ride back to turn left onto your intended route. Use appropriate signals to let other road users know where you intend to go, and observe your surroundings continually. Remember to keep moving and not

to hesitate during your manoeuvre as this helps you and your horse stay safe around potentially high volumes of traffic.

Roundabouts

Roundabouts can be tricky to negotiate from horseback as they require lots of observations and signalling in a short amount of time. When riding around a roundabout you should keep to the left and watch out for vehicles crossing your path when leaving or joining. If you have to stop at the roundabout before joining it then remember to carry out your observations before you stop. Once you have stopped, look right, left and take another look behind you to make sure it is safe to join the roundabout before moving off again. Look over your right shoulder and signal right as you ride past the exits you don't require. Look behind you and left past each junction so you are aware of the traffic at all times. Just before you reach the junction you wish to take, look all around you to make sure it is safe to exit the roundabout, signal left, check behind you one last time and then make your turn off the roundabout.

The *Highway Code* states that you should avoid roundabouts wherever possible.

Flared junctions

A flared junction looks like a T junction but widens on the left as you approach the white line. It is dangerous to position your horse into the side of a flared junction as a car may pull up on your right-hand side putting you and your horse in a very vulnerable position. To position yourself safely, stay on your line in the road rather than following the curve to the left. Halt before you reach the white line.

Stationary vehicles

Should you come across a parked or stationary vehicle out riding it is important to know how to pass it safely and with consideration to other road users. On approach, make sure you keep left but look behind you in good time to see if there is any traffic. You may need to stop and wait for traffic to pass you before you overtake the stationary vehicle. When it is safe, signal right, look behind you again, then move out and gradually pass the car.

> It is also possible that a car may be reversing as you approach it. This will be shown by the reversing light, which is white in colour and located on the back of the car near the brake lights.

Leave enough room for a car door to be opened between you and the stationary vehicle as you pass. Also be aware that pedestrians may walk out from in front of the car. Sudden movement or noise may come from inside the car, so stay alert. Gradually move back over to the left-hand side of the road, once you have good clearance of the vehicle.

More and more electric cars are on the road, they are usually quieter than normal vehicles, so you and your horse might be spooked. It would be a good idea to ensure you are observing at all times whilst riding out so you can be as prepared as possible.

Gritting Lorries

- Familiarise yourself with the gritting status of roads you use regularly and you may want to sign up to any notification service provided by your Highways Authority – this will allow you to lower the risk of meeting gritter lorries.

- Gritter lorries cannot miss sections of road in the salt distribution as to do so risks dangerous ice. Except on wide roads, the salt is sprayed over both lanes but not beyond the kerb. So you should move off the main carriageway and as far away from the gritting area, as possible.

- If you see that a gritter lorry is behind you, look for somewhere safe to step off the main carriageway. Turn your horse's head so that he can see the source of the noise/flashing lights.

- Once you have done so, signal to the driver that your horse is settled; they should then pass you slowly.

- We always recommend wearing appropriate high visibility clothing when riding out, this enables you to increase your conspicuity and visibility to all drivers.

If you have an incident with a gritter lorry that causes you concern please report it to the BHS Incident Website bhs.org.uk/reportanincident

Road works

You may come across road works, noisy machinery or frightening hazards such as bird scarers, bins or loud sports activities whilst out hacking, even on small country lanes. When approaching such a hazard, first look around you to see if there is any traffic. If there is, it is safer to stop before the hazard and let the traffic pass before attempting to ride past. If you can, try to get the operator's attention as they may turn off the machinery or stop what they

are doing while you ride past. If they do, remember to thank them for doing so. If your horse is reluctant to go past the hazard and you are in company, you could ask for a lead from the other horse. If you are by yourself and your horse is reluctant to go past try to turn his head away from the hazard as you approach and go past, however, if the horse is getting quite stressed you may need to consider an alternative route.

Find out more information and read our advice to drivers and horse riders.
bhs.org.uk/advice-for-Motorists

Summary

- You may come across traffic lights whilst out riding. Horse riders need to abide by the same road rules as other road users. Be aware of queuing traffic and try and avoid having cars on your nearside.

- Try to avoid roundabouts; however, should you need to ride on one, ensure you observe plenty of times and keep signalling to notify other road users where you intend to get to.

- Constantly assess your route: Expect the unexpected.

TRAINING TIPS

1. Be familiar with the sequence of traffic lights: when in a car see if you can guess the next set of lights likely to appear.

2. Practise riding around a parked car in a controlled situation.

3. When passing a hazard and returning back to the road remember to check over both shoulders for any road users.

Chapter 5

Riding Off the Road

Do I know what signs to look out for?

Below are examples that apply to England, Wales and Northern Ireland only. Please note for equestrian routes in Scotland refer to the Scottish Outdoor Access Code and the Land Reform [Scotland] Act 2003 and for Republic of Ireland please refer to the Rules of the Road. These can be found at bhs.org.uk/Scotland or bhs.org.uk/Ireland

Out riding you will come across paths marked with different colours known as 'waymarkers'. These take different forms, depending where you live, from paint splashes on trees to circular plastic discs with arrows. These will indicate where you and your horse can and can't go according to the law.

If you are unsure, please read the BHS guide on finding new places to ride and carriage drive at bhs.org.uk

Below is a snapshot of some of the most common signs and what they mean to you: please note these can differ slightly by highway authority.

 ● Footpath: may be used only by walkers unless you are aware of unrecorded higher user rights for the footpath or you have obtained the landowner's permission to ride on the footpath – **waymarked by a yellow arrow**.

 ● Bridleway: may be used on foot or on horseback; horses may be led and in some cases there is the right to drive other animals. Cyclists are also permitted, however they need to give way to horse riders and pedestrians – **waymarked by a blue arrow**.

 ● Restricted byway: may be used by bridleway users as well as horse-drawn vehicles. They are not permitted for use by mechanically propelled vehicles such as cars or motorbikes – **waymarked by a plum-coloured arrow**.

• Byway open to all traffic: may be used by bridleway users as well as any kind of wheeled vehicle, including motor cars, motorcycles and horse-drawn vehicles – **waymarked by a red arrow.**

 • Permissive or permitted routes: Routes for which the landowner has reached an agreement with the Authority to allow linear public access. This permission may be withdrawn or the route altered over time. Permission may be given subject to certain restrictions; it should not be assumed that there is horseback access across these routes – **waymarked by a white or a black arrow.**

It is important to remember to keep to the line of way (or permissive route) unless there is an obstruction.

Gates and obstacles – how do I approach a gate?

Opening and closing gates safely is an important skill for hacking. Whilst out riding you may come across a gate and it is important to remember if a gate is closed and you pass through it, you must close the gate behind you. Training your horse to be responsive to your aids to make small adjustments in his steps will help you when you come to manoeuvre around a gate. Being a 'good gate opener' is a great credit to you both.

Self-closing gates have become very popular with landowners to help control unwanted stock movement, so it has become crucial to be competent and safe when operating them as you may find yourself caught whilst going through.

The heels to hinges method

The recommended method is commonly called 'heels to hinges' because the horse faces away from the gate's hinges. It is believed to give the most control and the least chance of catching your tack on the gate or latch. Approach the gate's hinges and position the horse alongside the gate, 'heels to hinges', with the latch by the horse's shoulder and the horse's head and neck extending beyond the latch, parallel to the gate.

Gates that open away from the rider

1. With the horse standing parallel to the gate, heels to hinges, lean over to release the latch and push the gate open far enough to give a safe gap.

2. Back the horse up to bring his head into the opening, then turn and ride through the gap, bending the horse around your leg nearest the gate.

3. Turn round the end of the gate, push it closed and secure the latch.

Gates opening towards the rider

1. With the horse standing parallel to the gate, heels to hinges, lean over and open the latch, then move the horse sideways away from the gate while keeping one hand on the gate and opening it with you.

2. Move forwards and turn round the end of the gate when the opening is wide enough.

3. Once through the gateway, you may be able to move your hand along the gate towards the hinges, closing the gate behind you before backing up to secure the latch. Or you may need to turn the horse, heels to hinges, parallel to the gate and then move sideways while pulling the gate closed.

When NOT to use the 'heels to hinges' method

This method may not work if there is no space for the horse's head and neck beyond the latch, or insufficient space to come alongside the gate. Many riders manage to negotiate gates with the horse's head over the gate, but it is less safe as you will often need to swap hands, potentially losing control. There is a greater risk of the reins or martingale getting caught, and the gate or latch may hit the horse's head. Much depends on the latch mechanism – one that has to be held open while the gate clears it is more difficult to open when not parallel to the gate. Self-closing gates that swing quickly can be impossible with this method, or require several attempts, which can be tedious and time-consuming and will increase the risk of injury. Mastering the heels to hinges method generally improves the chance of coping with a gate where space is too tight because the horse is more responsive and the rider is more likely to retain control even in less-than-ideal conditions.

For more information please visit the Access Department of the BHS website and see their YouTube video 'How to open a gate safely'.

Open fields

Most land has to provide the owner with an income and on land that is not arable (i.e. used for crop growing) this is likely to include stock-keeping,

whether cattle, sheep, pigs or less common stock such as llamas or deer. Take some time to learn about farming operations and be sensitive to the needs of those managing land. There are certain things you can be aware of, or do, to ensure that you ride courteously across agricultural land and ensure ongoing access for all of us to enjoy with our horses:

- Keep your speed appropriate to the ground conditions; hooves can quickly damage ground in wet conditions. Common objections to equestrian routes include poached ground or riders 'galloping all over the place'. Make sure you know the law.

- In England, Wales and Northern Ireland where a public right of way is signposted or marked, you should not deviate from the route.

- Learn to recognise local crops in all stages of growth; remember that grass too is either a crop to be harvested or required for feed. Where an unfenced or equestrian route crosses a field of ungrazed grass in early summer, ride in single file if possible and certainly no more than two abreast, as it will be required for winter feed. Stubble may be sown with an under crop which can easily be damaged with a gallop. If you can, check with the landowner the preferred path to follow, if one isn't clearly marked.

- Be aware a tractor driver will not be able to hear you approach and if he is concentrating on operating the machinery behind him he may not immediately see you. Try to wait in a safe place until he has seen you and you can pass safely.

Guidelines for riding across open country

- If a legal line or path exists, do not stray from it (England and Wales only).

- Do not damage timber or hedgerows by jumping.

- Remember that horses' hooves can cause poaching when it's wet.

- Pay particular attention to protected areas that have historical or conservation significance and may be extremely sensitive to damage. If in any doubt you should avoid these areas.

- Always make sure that you can be seen by wearing the right kind of reflective or fluorescent equipment.

- Ride respectfully through Sites of Special Scientific Interest (SSSI) or areas of environmental conservation.

Consideration for the farmer

- Always leave a farm gate how you find it. If it is closed, make sure you close it behind you.

- Ride slowly past **all** stock.

- Do not deviate from the right of way or permitted route and always show regard for growing crops. Do not ride on cultivated land unless the legal right of way crosses it. Ensure you are riding responsibly at all times.

- Observe local bylaws. These are usually on display as you enter sites that have bylaws. If unsure inquire before riding, online.

How do I ride past livestock?

When riding through agricultural land it is very likely that you will come across livestock, and it is important for their safety, plus that of your horse and yourself that you know how to behave should you come into contact with them. Learning their characteristics helps you to react accordingly and avoid any unwanted distress or harm.

- Cattle are notoriously inquisitive and what may appear as aggression is commonly curiosity, especially if they are young, recently turned out or handled infrequently. Cattle are prey animals, like horses, and not usually aggressive, unless they are cows protecting calves or a bull protecting his cows, which require extra care. It might be best to avoid fields with a sign stating a bull is in the field. A group of young cattle can become very boisterous, with serious repercussions. Often cattle are let out in the spring once the grass is high enough. Passing through them calmly will ensure that they get used to horses and quieten down. Longhorn and Highland cattle are often used for conservation grazing. They may appear particularly menacing because of their long horns but they are among the most docile breeds. If you need to move cattle out of your way, walk towards them waving your arms or a stick and make loud noises, like clapping or tapping your leg (being mindful of the effect on your horse and anyone else with you). Overall, be firm and confident; expect them to move and most likely they will.

- Pigs have quite poor eyesight and are relatively slow-moving so tend to lose interest in nearby path users. They are usually confined by electric fencing, which should not cross a public right of way. However, horses can take a real dislike to them so be careful not to get too close.

- Loose horses can be the biggest problem if you encounter them whilst riding through a field. Being of the same species, there can be issues of territory and ownership that do not exist with other livestock. As with cattle, if you need to move loose horses out of your way, acting with firmness and confidence achieves the best results (be mindful of the effect on your own horse or companions). You may need to turn towards them repeatedly as you cross a field. Over time, if the equestrian route is well used, it is likely that loose horses will become uninterested in people passing through. Until that point though it is advisable to ride with someone else so that one rider can deter the horses while the other opens the gate. We strongly recommend against stallions being kept in fields through which rights of way pass but it is not prohibited and does happen. If you are aware of stallions near popular equestrian routes and you own or ride a mare, you will need to observe closely when she is in season and avoid routes near stallions at this time. Even a stallion in an adjacent field to a mare in season may create a dangerous situation.

- Sheep are most likely to avoid horses and riders or run from people or dogs. However, they can easily be panicked by you and your horse, running blindly into corners of the field or fences, particularly if you are going faster than a walk, which in turn can cause them to become panic-stricken and at risk of aborting if they are in lamb. Be very careful at gates to ensure that sheep, especially lambs, do not dash through while the gate is open; this is most likely if they feel cornered or separated from the flock. Ewes (female sheep) with lambs may try to protect their young, perhaps by stamping their feet, but are very rarely aggressive. Never trot or canter through fields of sheep unless they are very distant. If sheep become unsettled, lambs may become separated from their mothers, making a lot of work for the farmer to pair them up again, with the risk of the mothers rejecting their lambs. Rams (male sheep) can be aggressive and should be treated with caution. They are most likely to be out with ewes during autumn and winter.

For further information please read online 'Advice on riding through cattle, other livestock and horses' produced by the BHS Access department, found at bhs.org.uk

- Bird scarers can frequently be placed in locations near where you ride, emitting loud bangs, which frighten away birds from eating seeds, but are also potentially frightening to your horse. We promote the NFU guidance which can be shown to landowners.

If you have an incident with a bird scarer, please let us know
bhs.org.uk/reportanincident

Sharing routes with others

It is likely that you will meet other people including carriage drivers, walkers with dogs, young families with pushchairs, cyclists or small motorised mobility scooters. Dog walkers should ensure their dog is under close control, and you may need to stop and wait for the dog to be put on a lead before it is safe to pass. Keep your speed appropriate to your surroundings. Also, be aware that other people may be frightened of horses, so pass them slowly and politely. Whenever possible, acknowledge courtesy shown by other users with a wave, smile or a thank you.

Equestrians, cyclists, walkers and wheelchair users are all vulnerable road users and have the right to be on byways, bridleways and roads. We encourage all groups to work together so all can access safe and enjoyable off-road riding.

A few helpful pointers for horse riders:

- Be aware at all times and expect the unexpected.
- Many people are not familiar with horses and may not know how to behave around them.
- Be nice – say hi.

Be nice - say hi

We are working closely with Cycling UK, British Cycling and British Triathlon to teach cycling groups and promote safer riding for all users by working together. The 'Be Nice Say Hi Initiative' encourages cyclists to alert their presence to the rider, and for the rider to acknowledge the cyclist. For more information, or to request some leaflets to drop in at your local cycle group, visit bhs.org.uk/safety

Wheelchair users

As with other road users, slow to a walk to pass. Pass with plenty of space as wheelchair users will find it difficult to move out of the way quickly should your horse spook. You will also have to be prepared to halt your horse to allow the wheelchair user to pass as they may not be able to divert their route if there are obstructions or uneven ground ahead.

We work with Disabled Ramblers and The Experience Community to aid and educate users of shared spaces. View our latest video on passing users with wheelchairs or mobility vehicles at bhs.org.uk

Please read the BHS leaflet on responsible riding and carriage driving at: bhs.org.uk

Remember, if there is a problematic gate on an equestrian route that is unsafe or unusable by horse riders you can report it to your local council. Find your local council contact details at gov.uk/find-local-council

What should I do if I come across an obstruction or poorly maintained route?

Report it! Please don't just ignore it or forget about it if the route is impassable. Our volunteers can help you to liaise with the people responsible in your local area to get the problem resolved. Contact our access department for help on 02476 840515.

On occasion you may meet people who, for whatever reason, act aggressively towards you and your horse. Riders themselves can be surprised into acting aggressively, perhaps if someone has unsettled their horse. The best rule in such situations is not to lose your temper, and to apologise for speaking brusquely, even if you're convinced that you're in the right. The real rights and wrongs of the matter can often be resolved at a later, calmer, time. Please see the online leaflet 'Dealing with confrontation' from the BHS Access department at: bhs.org.uk

Dogs

Loose dogs or dogs not under control can be a common concern for riders, either with walkers or in gardens that you ride past. The instincts to chase and hunt usually remain even in a pet dog. Some dogs will never have seen a horse before, which could result in aggression or chasing. Other dogs may see a horse and want to play, which the horse may not understand or may misinterpret as a threat.

Below are some suggestions to minimise the risk of an incident when you come across dogs:

- Try to socialise your horse with dogs so he does not react to their presence.

- Keep your horse as calm as possible when passing dogs.

- Slow to a walk, and communicate with the dog owner at the earliest opportunity. They may not have seen you – particularly if you are approaching from behind.

- Give dogs that appear nervous a wide berth so they do not feel threatened.

- Wear high visibility equipment so dog owners can see you as soon as possible and take control of their dog.

- If riding in a group, go past in single file, at walk.

- Always thank dog owners who keep control and allow you to pass them safely.

- Do not shout or wave your arms around.

- If necessary, stop to allow an excited dog to be caught.

Understanding dog behaviour around horses

Follow these simple steps to keep you safe:
- Stay calm
- Protect young or vulnerable riders
- Allow the horse to defend himself

If an incident has occurred:
- Ensure the safety of your horse and yourself
- Try to take contact details from the dog owner
- Report to the police, if necessary
- Report to bhs.org/reportanincident

For further advice to reduce your risk of dog incidents, see our website: bhs.org.uk/reportanincident

Disease prevention

When riding out you may come across other horses and animals either being ridden or perhaps loose in fields. A basic approach should be adopted to protect your horse from illness and to avoid spreading disease. You don't know if the horses you see are carrying an illness, disease or infection. Although most horses that are sick would usually be rested in stables, many horses can be a carrier for a disease and not show any outward signs of it, so it is important you are wary of all unknown horses you meet on your ride. Disease can be spread directly between horses, commonly by physical touch (touching noses, grooming each other), touching an object the carrier horse has touched (for example a fence post or stable door), sharing water with carrier horses or by water droplets in the air. Disease can also be spread indirectly from a person handling different horses, so avoid touching horses you do not know or wash your hands in between handling different horses.

Many horses are inquisitive and if you ride past a field of loose horses it's likely that at least one will come up to the fence line or boundary. Keep your horse moving to prevent him from touching noses with any others that want to say hello and try not to let your horse have a scratch on a fence post or gate on the edge of the field. If you come across a water bucket or trough don't allow your horse to drink from it. You don't know who else has shared the water or how long it's been since it was cleaned. The bacteria that cause strangles can survive in water for several weeks.

You should also ensure your horse is vaccinated against equine flu and tetanus (although tetanus is not infectious it can be fatal). Tetanus is a bacterium found in soil and easily preventable with a vaccination programme. Contact your vet for further advice. If you are aware of any infectious disease outbreak at yards that you pass along your planned route we would recommend avoiding that area until the all clear has been given.

> For more information about protecting your horse from disease, please visit the welfare pages on our website: bhs.org.uk/advice-and-information

Poisonous plants

You should be aware of the common poisonous plants that can be found as it is often tempting for a horse to try to grab a mouthful as he walks past a hedge or tree. The general rule would be not to let your horse eat anything on a ride out, even a mouthful, as this small amount can be fatal depending on the plant. Some common plants found in the UK and Republic of Ireland are as follows:

Ragwort

Ragwort is a common weed poisonous to horses and grows throughout the British Isles. It is very likely you will see ragwort on a ride out. A small amount will not be fatal, but eaten over a period of time can lead to liver damage and death. Ragwort is controlled by two Acts and if you come across it

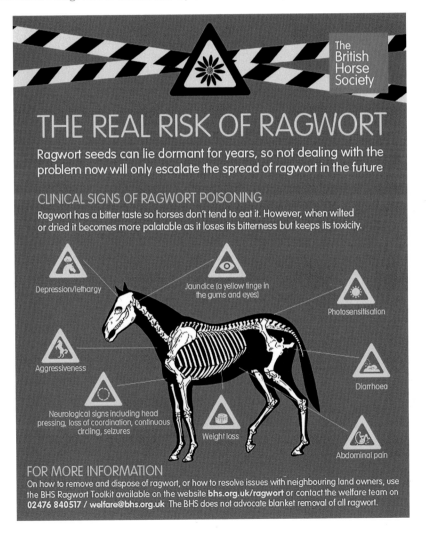

growing near to, or in fields
grazed by horses or used to
produce forage such as hay,
you could report it. See our
ragwort tool kit for further
information: bhs.org.uk/
advice-and-information

Foxglove
A common garden plant, but it can be found in fields and woodland. Foxglove
can be fatal for horses. Signs of foxglove poisoning include contracting pupils,
breathing difficulties and convulsions with death after only a few hours.

Deadly nightshade
This plant can be found in open fields, pasture, woodland and along the
roadside. Although not fatal, poisoning can cause unconsciousness, dilation of
the pupils and convulsions.

Hemlock
A common weed found in woodland and fields. Hemlock poisoning is fast-
acting and usually brings death within a few hours. Early signs are excessive
salivation, muscle weakness and tremors and disorientation.

Trees and shrubs

There are also a number of hedges and trees that are poisonous to horses
that are often used within field boundaries of farmland or in gardens and
woodland.

Sycamore
Most likely recognised by the
helicopter seeds that fall in
autumn, sycamore seeds and
seedlings that grow during
the spring-time and can cause
muscle tremors, reluctance
to walk and stiffness and
breathing difficulties. It is
a disease called Atypical
Myopathy and it can be fatal.

Yew

Yew poses a serious risk to horses; there have been many reported cases of death where horses have eaten a small amount of the tree. Yew contains a number of toxins, poisoning can occur at any time of the year and all parts of the tree (except the fleshy part of the fruit) are poisonous. It's safe to say that you need to ensure your horse does not consume yew, even if it is dried as it still remains poisonous. Signs of poisoning include restlessness, trembling, weakness, incoordination, changes to the pulse rate, diarrhoea, colic and breathing difficulties. Death can occur suddenly.

The list of poisonous plants, shrubs and trees is extensive and horse owners must make themselves aware of what is unsafe for their horses. A brief guide like this cannot mention every poisonous species, although a great deal of information is available on the internet and in reference books. Further advice can be sought from the BHS Welfare Department.

Wind turbines

Riders with experience of wind turbines, whose horses have reacted to them, believe this is because of the associated noise, movement or shadows. However, we have received many reports about horses being completely undisturbed by turbines. Most wary horses become less anxious with familiarity and sensitive handling, so do not assume that wind turbines will cause you a problem. As with most hazards, there may be a correlation between your horse's reaction and your expectation of a reaction, so it is important to ride positively and confidently while remaining sensitive to your horse's response. Keep calm and relaxed, quietly reassuring your horse, just as you would in any other situation.

Tips on how to ride amongst wind turbines

- Watch your horse's ears; they will tell you which direction your horse thinks a sound or potential hazard is coming from, and any reaction is likely to be made in the opposite direction.

- It may help to turn the horse towards the turbine to help him identify the source of the noise.

- If shadows cross your path, and if your route allows it, try riding in a direction that makes the shadows appear to move away from you, making them appear less threatening to your horse.

- Weather can change quickly and the wind can rise suddenly, especially on high ground. If you are riding by turbines on a large wind farm when the wind rises, several turbines may come into motion together, which could frighten any horse. Be particularly alert to weather conditions and plan alternative routes that avoid the wind farm if necessary.

Solar panel farms

Lines of linked panels will normally be fixed facing south and tilted at approximately 45 degrees. Glare from the panels is unlikely to be a problem as you are moving, but it is something to be aware of.

The panels do not make any noise or movement, unlike wind turbines, however if you ride past them in wet weather you may hear a very subtle sound as the rain lands on the panel.

If you are planning to ride past a solar or wind farm for the first time, as with other potential hazards, try to ride with an older or more experienced horse and rider. This will give both you and your horse a boost of confidence should you become a little unsure when riding past the solar panels. Reassure your horse with your voice as you pass. He will take a lot of confidence from hearing your voice. Remember to have an alternative route in mind should your horse get too upset to go past.

For further information about wind turbines and solar farms please visit: bhs.org.uk

Summary

- It is always best to open a gate on horseback using the heels to hinge method if you are able to.

- Different colour waymarks let you know who can and cannot ride along the path.

- Always report unsafe gates or impassable routes to your local authority. If you need any help then contact the BHS Access department who can support you.

- Should you find yourself having to deal with an incident involving a dog you should remember to: stay calm, protect young or vulnerable riders and allow the horse to defend himself.

- If a dog appears nervous, try and give it a wide berth and always walk past it whilst communicating.

- You may come across lots of different livestock when riding out. Your horse might react differently to different animals and being aware of this can help you deal with a situation should it arise.

- Always be mindful when riding across agricultural land that crops may be growing and you should keep as close to the fence as possible unless a path has been clearly marked out for you by the farmer.

- You should always leave gates as you find them.

- Be aware when walking past wind turbines on your horse for the first time; he might be interested or spooky. It would be best to ride out with a confident/more experienced horse the first time.

- Solar panels may also take your horse by surprise if you are riding past these for the first time so we do recommend you ride with a more experienced/confident horse.

TRAINING TIPS

1. Practise with a friend opening and closing a gate on horseback, practising the heels to hinge method. Always ensure you are in a safe environment before starting.

2. Be aware of how to navigate when riding out. Plan your route and carry a map if riding somewhere new, so you will be ready when out riding.

3. If you can, try to get your horse used to dogs in a controlled environment. This should help your horse be less spooky should you come across them when riding out.

4. When out riding, or in the car, have a look at what livestock you can see and think about how your horse might react to them.

5. Before riding out on a route where you think solar panels or a wind farm has been recently built, it might be a good idea to go in your car to scout out where they are. This will help with planning your route and ensuring both you and your horse are safe if he was to spook.

Chapter 6

Riding on a Beach

Riding on beaches and estuaries

Riding on beaches and estuaries

Many riders aspire to ride on a coast and it can be a wonderful experience for both you and your horse.

> If you live very far from a beach, or do not own a horse, consider visiting a BHS approved centre near the coast that offers beach riding, listed here: bhs.org.uk/enjoy-riding/find-a-place-to-ride

Planning your visit

Do your homework before setting off, including checking that riding is permitted at your intended destination as it is not allowed on all beaches. Riding may only be allowed at certain times, or in certain areas of the beach. Boundaries may not always be obvious, so research where you are allowed and where you are not. It's also essential to check the tides, an issue unique to beach riding. Tides can come in very quickly and cut off your planned route, leaving you stranded. In the event that you get into difficulty, call 999 to

> Tide timetables are available online, from the council and often local shops.

contact the coastguard and make sure you can give accurate details about your whereabouts. As the tide goes out, it may leave slippery surface conditions, or incredibly dangerous hazards like sinking sand. Stay alert and look out for warning signs. Be careful not to disturb plants and wildlife as this may prevent riding access in the future.

We publish details of UK beaches that welcome horses and highlight any restrictions: bhs.org.uk

First time at the beach

A horse paying his first visit to the beach may be on his toes. Beaches are large, open spaces, often quite windy, and there may be more people and dogs around than your horse is used to. Cantering across the beach can be a memorable moment and a lot of fun, but do be aware of your surroundings, other beach users and stay safe and in control.

It may seem obvious but a key difference between beach riding and hacking out on equestrian routes is the sand. Sand consistency can vary suddenly from quite deep to soft or very hard. All of these can cause injury to a horse if you do not ride carefully and at an appropriate speed. It is advisable to walk and trot initially to check the surface. Also look out for possible holes, debris and the occasional sandcastle!

Common beach activities you may come across during your visit are picnicking families, long-line fishing, sand yachting, parasailing and more. These may be activities your horse is not used to and could cause him to worry. Try if possible to check with the locals what activity is likely to happen when – this will help you to avoid popular times or areas and make the most of your trip to the beach.

Estuaries

Estuaries appear where rivers meet the sea and they can provide excellent riding opportunities. However, they can also be unpredictable places. You need to be cautious and have some awareness of the different ground conditions you may come across. Estuaries are often home to many forms of wildlife, some of which may be protected species. Look out for advisory signs and if you see flocks of birds feeding take care not to disturb or startle them. Equestrian access and use of estuaries will be threatened if local wildlife regulations are not adhered to, so please be mindful of this when visiting and make sure it is a positive experience for all. You may come across sand dunes and salt marshes during your visit to an estuary; these are fragile environments and riding through them should be avoided if possible for conservation reasons.

The sea

The movement and noise of breaking waves can be daunting to a horse who has not seen the sea before. Even if your horse is usually confident in water, they may need a bit of time to become accustomed to it. When you first enter the sea, ride slowly but confidently. Approach from an angle rather than head on, so that if your horse spooks at the waves, he is more likely to shy away from the water than attempt to rear. Approaching alongside the shallows often encourages nervous horses to get their feet wet. We do not recommend riding in water if you cannot see the bottom; there may be hidden debris or rocks, which could cause an injury. Seaweed can be very slippery, so try to avoid riding over it. We do not recommend taking your horse out far in the water until he swims. Horses find it difficult to turn in water and once you add the extra weight of tack and rider, plus the difficulty of waves and choppy water, it is too easy for your horse to get into trouble.

As ever, fluorescent or reflective clothing is important; tides can come in fast and fog can descend very quickly when riding on or close to the sea. High visibility clothing will allow you to be easily spotted by other beach users.

Remember to note that some beaches require you to remove your horse's droppings; it is good practice to do so on all beaches. Try to remember to take a scoop with you in your trailer or horse box.

Summary

- Riding on the beach can be great fun, especially with friends. However, ensure you check up on the tide times before leaving and any restrictions on the beach.

- Riding your horse in the sea can be a very enjoyable experience. However, you should never enter water where you cannot see the bottom and never go out of your horse's depth.

TRAINING TIPS

1. When walking out on the beach be familiar with the different sand textures, as some might be too deep to ride through.

Chapter 7

Rules of the School

Arena riding – the universal code of conduct
riding at home or away

Arena riding – the universal code of conduct riding at home or away

Many of us will use arenas at some point: this could be a group lesson with a coach, shared use with liveries or in a warm-up arena at a competition. No matter the situation, it is useful to know the code of conduct for arena riding, outlined below. If all riders follow the universal code, you can all enjoy the arena safely and respectfully.

- Always knock before entering an indoor arena or catch the attention of a rider in an outdoor arena; this is to warn anyone inside or riding that you are coming in, and allow them the chance to slow down or halt while you open the door or gate.

- Riders sharing an arena should always pass each other 'left to left', i.e. left shoulder to left shoulder, to avoid confusion and accidental obstructions.

- When riding in a group, try to leave one horse's length between you and the horse in front.

- Riders sharing an arena may wish to walk, trot and canter at different times. Anyone walking should use the inside track, and allow others in faster gaits to pass on the outside track.

- When jumping, be sure that both your take-off and landing path are clear before you approach a fence. In warm-up arenas at competitions (whether affiliated or unaffiliated), you always jump with the red wing or flag on your right, so all traffic goes in the same direction.

- A red ribbon tied in a horse's tail indicates a horse that may kick. A green ribbon in a horse's tail indicates that it is a young horse, so be mindful on how these horses may react when being passed.

- Other common rules include picking up any droppings your horse has done before leaving the arena. If you are on your own, it is acceptable to take your horse back to the stable first and come back to do this. Some centres require you to pick your horse's feet out before you leave the arena to try to minimise the dispersal of arena surface.

Summary

- When riding with others, you should always pass left shoulder to left shoulder and ensure you allow one horse's length between you and the horse in front.

- If you are walking whilst riding with others, you should always take the inside track.

TRAINING TIPS

1. When riding in a lesson or with other riders practise being aware of others. Communicate with other riders to let them know where you plan to ride and practise riding on an inner track.

Chapter 8

Low-Flying Aircraft and Drones

What can I do if I come across
a low-flying aircraft or drone?

It is essential for military aircraft to train at low-level so they can support operational forces. Military pilots are well trained to avoid flying over horse riders wherever possible. Increase your chances of being seen early by you and your horse wearing high visibility clothing that can be seen from overhead, such as a sheet for your horse and a hat silk and vest for yourself.

A pilot can see a rider wearing high visibility clothing up to half a mile (0.8km) sooner than one riding without it.

If they do not see you until the last moment, the aircraft will usually continue flying over you but stop any planned manoeuvre, which will be less frightening to you and your horse than the pilot taking last-minute action.

What can I do if I come across a low-flying aircraft or drone?

Your horse has exceptionally good hearing and can pick up sounds that humans cannot. Their highly mobile ears enable them to pick up faint noises up to 4km (2.5 miles) away, so your horse will probably hear a helicopter or low-flying aircraft before you do. If he starts to become worried or anxious, reassure him by talking to him. Running your hand along his neck can also be comforting and have a calming influence. It is really important that you as the rider, remain calm and ride positively, trying to keep your horse listening to you until the aircraft has passed.

You can find out when training is planned for most areas of the UK by calling freephone 0800 515544. When pre-planned exercises and other events are scheduled, notifications are posted on the local RAF station website and in local media.

Drones come in a huge and diverse range of forms. These vary from the small, hand-held radio-controlled versions, as an alternative to model aircraft and are used in the owners' gardens and open spaces, right through to the ones that are being used in industry and by an ever-widening range of businesses.

It's important for riders to have some understanding of drones and the legal restrictions surrounding them, should they be encountered when out riding. This awareness should help you to reassure your horse, and reduce the risk of him becoming spooked by such random flying objects. To find out more visit bhs.org.uk/drones

If you are involved in an incident please report it to us by completing the general incident form on the website and sending into us at bhs.org.uk/reportanincident

Summary

- Low-flying aircraft may spook your horse as they may be very loud. To give yourself the best chance to be seen you should wear high visibility clothing. The pilot should then hopefully be able to re-direct their flight path to avoid you and make it less frightening for you and your horse if seen in time. If a pilot sees you too late it is safer to continue on a flight path to avoid 'blade slapping.' If this happens keep calm and reassure your horse.

TRAINING TIPS

1. To find out where training may take place in the UK you can freephone 0800 515544. This will help you avoid their training times/scheduled events.

Chapter 9

The Ride Safe Award

Ride Safe Award training guidance

Ride Safe Award training guidance

We recommend that you contact an Accredited Professional Ride Safe Trainer, who will be able to explain how much training you will need based on your current level of riding or driving ability. It is usual to attend a series of training sessions with an Accredited Professional or British Horse Society Approved Centre before undertaking the Ride Safe Award.

You can also take part in the Riding Out Safely Silver Challenge Award. This will give you great training ready for the award. It will cover:

- Gaining the confidence and skills to ride safely on roads and when out and about.

- Knowing how to plan routes and prepare yourself and your horse to enjoy the countryside.

- How to ride in an enclosed arena with other riders.

- How to ride with the reins in one hand.

- Checks to make before setting off.

- How to request other route users to slow down or stop.

Booking your Ride Safe Award assessment day

To find dates for training and assessment in your local area, please visit our website: bhs.org.uk/pathways or email pathways@bhs.org.uk with any questions.

We recommend that you allow at least two months for training when you are looking to select your assessment date.

When you have decided on your preferred assessment date, please telephone one of our helpful team within the Education Department on 02476 840508, who will help you to complete your booking and can also give you details on training in your local area.

What to expect on your Ride Safe Award assessment day

As you near the date of your assessment day for your Ride Safe Award you will be given advice on what time to arrive at the centre and where to meet your assessor(s). On the day you will be given a candidate number and will usually be in a group of up to six, with a nominated assessor who will support you throughout the award. Our assessors are all friendly and approachable, with a passion for improving safety of all riders and horses.

You will then have your hat checked to make sure it is up to date with current standards and have a discussion with your assessor around general aspects of riding safely and the relevance of the appropriate sections of the *Highway Code* to horse riders.

In your group, you will continue with the award by taking your horse into an enclosed space, where you will be asked to lead him to a mounting block and then mount with due consideration for others around you. The arena may be set up to simulate a road environment.

Your group will ride together in walk and trot, for approximately 10-15 minutes so that you can demonstrate that you are safe, in control of your horse, and can ride with consideration for others in an enclosed environment such as an arena. You will be asked to show basic signals and manoeuvres as if you were on a road.

During this time your assessor will discuss with you relevant points of riding safely in different situations. This is to ensure that you will be safe to go out on the road in the next section of the assessment and that you are secure in the saddle. You will be asked to make an emergency dismount and lead your horse as if you were on a road.

After this you will walk (on foot) the road route with your assessor where you will be asked for comments relating to the road route before riding it, either individually or in pairs at the discretion of your assessor and centre.

If you have any questions regarding the Ride Safe Award or would like to discuss it further, please get in touch with a member of the BHS Education Team on 02476 840508.

Chapter 10

How The British Horse Society Supports You

How The British Horse Society supports you

Access & Rights of Way Department

The Access Team work to protect, extend and promote all safe off-road routes for riders and carriage drivers throughout the UK. We work pro-actively with other user groups such as Ramblers, Cycling England and Disabled Ramblers, the Experience Community and landowners including National Trust, MoD, Natural England, etc. There is a great network of trained Access and Bridleway Officers covering the UK who work to protect and extend access in their local areas. There are also a great number of BHS affiliated Equestrian Access Groups who champion equestrian access in their areas and often organise fun rides out. If you would like to get more involved in protecting or extending equestrian access in your area, please contact our Access Team on 02476 840515.

In England, did you know that in the year 2026 all incorrectly recorded routes on the definitive map will be lost forever? This includes a great proportion of the routes currently used by equestrians. We are leading a campaign to ensure all such routes are legally recorded before 2026. To find out if your local BHS needs your help on this, please contact the Access Team on 02476 840515.

Love hacking, love the BHS!

Ride Out UK is our annual campaign which aims to raise awareness about the need for safe off-road routes and encouraging people to explore the great outdoors whilst raising money for Paths for Communities. This fund provides grants to restore, improve and create multi-user routes around the UK.

The BHS Paths for Communities Fund

Do you know of a route that could be opened for equestrian access; or of a problem such as a boggy surface or difficult gate, that could potentially be resolved with some money? The BHS Paths for Communities Fund aims to expand and protect equestrian access in the UK. Find out more about applying to the fund with a project, or raising money for the fund at bhs.org. uk/access-and-bridleways/funds-and-fundraising

If you are keen to learn more about protecting the routes where you live for future generations, consider attending one of the ARoW training days held across the country, listed on the BHS website. You could also sign up to our monthly ARoW update to stay in the know with what is happening on important access matters that could affect your riding out. Email access@bhs.org.uk to subscribe.

Welfare Department

The BHS Welfare Team is striving to make a difference for horses throughout the UK by providing advice and support to their owners and guardians. As well as our team based at HQ and our external Field Officers, we are proud to have a vast nationwide network of approximately 200 equine specialist volunteer Welfare Advisers.

A free helpline is available to anybody who has a welfare concern for horses they are worried about. We are also happy to provide advice and support on a wide range of topics and confidential, empathic support through our Friends at the End scheme.

Our proactive work includes our Healthcare & Education Clinics and Horse Health Days. We collaborate with a huge number of organisations to continually improve UK equine welfare.

If you are interested in becoming a volunteer Welfare Adviser, or would like copies of our advisory literature, contact the Welfare Team on welfare@bhs. org.uk, call 02476 840517 or visit bhs.org.uk

You can support the BHS in its welfare work by taking out a Helping Horses membership. Please contact the Membership Team on 02476 840506 for more information.

Safety Department

The BHS Safety Department works to ensure that all equestrians and their horses are as safe as possible at all times. The department's work is both proactive and reactive to members' and equestrians' concerns. We have partners who work with us on road safety, dog incidents, low-flying aircraft, bicycles, fireworks and drones, in fact anything that may call the safety of horses and equestrians into question. We also work alongside the Police, Government and the RAF and have a network of volunteer Equestrian Safety Advisers all over the UK. Our volunteer Equestrian Safety Advisers can provide a local response in the first instance in conjunction with the BHS HQ Team, who support all equestrians and owners in any way they can. If you would like to speak to a member of our Safety Team please get in touch via email at safety@bhs.org.uk or phone on 02476 840516.

Please remember that any incident that has caused concern, even a near miss, should be reported to bhs.org.uk/reportanincident

Education Department

What is an Accredited Professional and
Accredited Professional Ride Safe Trainer?

BHS
Accredited
Professional

An Accredited Professional is a qualified riding coach who meets the highest professional standards within the industry, and is approved and accredited by The British Horse Society. As the largest professional body representing equestrian coaches globally, Accredited Professionals create the benchmark for the industry.

The Accredited Professional community facilitates a professional coaching community connecting people, ideas and resources to embed world-class standards, drives continual professional development and promotes innovation in equestrian coaching. Accredited Professionals are located throughout the UK. Please visit the BHS website to find an Accredited Professional near you.

Learn how to care for horses, develop hands-on, practical skills and get stuck in with the day-to-day tasks

If you're looking for a strong bond with a healthy, happy horse, the Challenge Awards are perfect for you.

It doesn't matter what previous experience you have with horses, or if you're a complete beginner. All you need is enthusiasm and a love for horses! You do not even need to own your own horse.

You will receive expert guidance and support from BHS Approved Coaches and they will help you work towards and achieve your personal goals. You will be encouraged to enhance your knowledge at your own pace and advance on areas that are important to you!

But most importantly, you'll have fun along the way! Remember, there are no time limits, or constraints to complete an award, so you can work at your own pace to achieve your goals.

For more information please look on the website bhs.org.uk/challengeawards or contact the education team on 02476 840508.

Appendix

Horse sense

What is the *Highway Code*
and why do I need to know about it?

HORSE SENSE: Equestrian access in Scotland

Under the Land Reform (Scotland) Act 2003, horse riders and carriage drivers enjoy equal rights of access as walkers, cyclists and other non-motorised users to most land and inland water, day or night, provided that they exercise their rights responsibly. Land managers in turn are obliged to respect equestrian access rights and take proper account of the right of responsible access in managing their land. Detailed guidance can be found in the **Scottish Outdoor Access Code** and on The **British Horse Society Scotland (BHSS)** website.

Who do access rights apply to?

Individual horse riders and carriage drivers, as well as groups of individuals riding together can access most land without the need to seek permission. Access rights include commercial equestrian access such as pony trekking, provided the person exercising the right could carry on the activity other than commercially or for profit. BHSS recommends that as a matter of courtesy, all commercial operators and anyone organising an event should contact land owners and managers. Some activities require permission from the land owner/manager such as for repetitive schooling, or to use facilities such as custom-made gallops or cross-country jumps.

Where do rights of responsible equestrian access apply?

While paths and tracks provide the basic framework for off-road access; access rights also apply to other land.

LAND USE	ACCESS RIGHTS WITH A HORSE INCLUDE	ACCESS RIGHTS DON'T INCLUDE
CEREAL FRUIT OR VEGETABLE CROPS	Margins, headlands and endrigs of fields in which crops are growing or have been sown (but only in single file and if ground conditions allow). Stubble. Grass strips.	Fields in which crops have been sown or are growing.
GRASS BEING GROWN OR MANAGED FOR HAY OR SILAGE	Grass at an early stage of growth.	Grass at a large stage of growth (ankle deep).
HILLS, MOUNTAINS, MOORLAND	Rough grazing, moorland, unfenced land.	-
GRASSLAND GRAZED BY LIVESTOCK OR BEING USED FOR OTHER PURPOSES	Enclosed fields, rough grazing and other ground on which cattle, sheep, deer or other livestock are grazing (see advice overleaf).	-
WOODLAND AND FORESTS	Woodland and forests.	Areas where felling or extraction is actively happening.
BEACHES, LOCH SHORES, RIVERBANKS, CANAL TOWPATHS	Beaches, loch shores, riverbanks, water margins, canal towpaths.	-
BUILDINGS, STEADINGS, HOUSES	Established rights of way or specifically signed paths and tracks through steadings.	Land on which there is a house or other buildings, including tracks through steadings where there is no right of way or specially signed path, and land immediately surrounding buildings sufficient to ensure reasonable privacy.
GARDENS, SPORTS PITCHES	Grass sports or playing fields while not in use (but horses need to go around the edge and only without causing damage).	All private gardens. Land in use for a recreational purpose.
GOLF COURSES	Paths through or around golf courses, to cross over the land.	Greens, tees, fairways.

Supported by Scottish Natural Heritage

HORSE SENSE: See it from each other's point of view

WHAT ARE THE RESPONSIBILITIES OF LAND MANAGERS?

Take equestrian access rights into account when managing land.

Do not purposefully or unreasonably prevent, hinder, deter or interfere with responsible equestrian access, on or off paths and tracks. This means you shouldn't obstruct access, discourage or intimidate riders or carriage drivers.

Avoid locking gates on routes which riders use or might want to use. Where it is necessary to lock a gate temporarily to prevent illegal vehicular access, or where there is risk of livestock straying, provide a suitable alternative alongside.

Use the least restrictive option possible when replacing gates or erecting or replacing field boundary fencing or walls, particularly at intersections with paths and tracks. Self-closing bridlegates are ideal, but BHSS are happy to advise on other options.

Avoid obstructing paths and tracks by leaving machinery or dumping material without sufficient space for horses to pass alongside.

If you do have to temporarily restrict access, use signage and good communication to explain why and for how long, and clearly sign a suitable alternative route for horse riders as well as others enjoying outdoor access. Keep any restrictions to the minimum area and duration.

Warning signs about potential hazards (e.g. bulls, spraying) need to make clear when the risk applies and be removed when the risk is over.

Remember that fly-tipping, vandalism and anti-social behaviour are nothing to do with equestrian access. If you need to take action to address these issues, make sure you leave sufficient space alongside to allow legitimate access on foot, cycle or horse. Bear in mind that a regular throughflow of walkers and riders may help discourage the culprits of illegal activity who won't want to risk being seen.

WHAT ARE THE RESPONSIBILITIES OF HORSE RIDERS AND CARRIAGE DRIVERS?

You are responsible for yourself and your horse and for controlling your horse in any situation you may meet while out riding or carriage driving. It is up to you to decide whether a steep path or field of cows is safe to ride through, based on the abilities and experience of yourself and your horse.

Road Traffic Act 1988, in England and Wales a person who causes or permits a dog to be on a designated road without the dog being held on a lead is guilty of an offence.

Remember that farmers, foresters and others are making their living from the land **so don't interfere unreasonably with land management** or disturb those who live there.

Follow any reasonable advice or signage (provided it complies with the Land Reform Act) and leave all gates as you find them.

Take particular care through livestock, especially fields with cows and calves, or horses. Use an alternative route if possible or keep a safe distance and pass at a walk.

Enjoy your riding but restrict your speed to the ground conditions, a safe stopping distance, and how far you can see ahead.

Be prepared to alter your route if ground conditions are not suitable, or to avoid land management activities like: shooting, stalking, ploughing, crop spraying, gathering livestock. Check where stalking is taking place on: **www.outdooraccess-scotland.com/Practical-guide/public/heading-for-the-scottish-hills.**

Avoid areas created or managed for wildlife such as beetle banks, or sensitive bird-nesting habitat, particularly in the breeding season.

Riding on wet, boggy or soft ground can churn up paths and tracks. Look behind you – if you are leaving deep hoofprints, you are not riding responsibly.

Think about the cumulative impact of riding in a group, or repeatedly using the same route and your impact on other people, wildlife, livestock and the trail surface.

Respect others enjoying outdoor access. Horses can be very intimidating, particularly to the young, old and physically less agile, and to dogs. Always pass other people and vehicles at a walk, allow plenty of space, and be prepared to dismount or wait for others to pass if required.

Whenever possible **move your horse off the path before he goes to the toilet.** On well used routes or near houses, dismount and kick dung off the path (provided it's safe to do so).

BE SAFE AND BE SEEN: KEEP YOUR WITS ABOUT YOU AND WEAR HIGH VISIBILITY.

BE COURTEOUS: A FRIENDLY WAVE IS ALWAYS WELCOME.

For further guidance on riding on field headlands and field margins, towpaths, beaches or through livestock, and on disease prevention or dung, or if you're organising an event or running a business that involves equestrian access, see: **www.bhsscotland.org.uk/resources.html**

What is the *Highway Code* and why do I need to know about it?

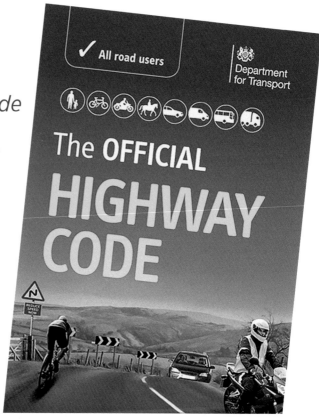

The *Highway Code* is an official set of rules and guidance for every road user in England, Scotland, Wales and Northern Ireland (please see specific *Highway Code*) whether they are a driver, motorcyclist, cyclist, horse rider or pedestrian. It exists to make sure that all road users are aware of the law when using the roads and ultimately to try to keep road users safe. We highly recommend that you read it before you go out on the road with your horse. It is also available online.

For the Republic of Ireland please visit the Road Safety Authority website as your primary road safety organisation – The *Rules of the Road* are equivalent to the *Highway Code* in the Republic of Ireland and can be found at bhs.org.uk The section on 'People in charge of animals – horse-drawn vehicles, riding or leading horses and driving animals on the road' is particularly useful.

Rider-specific section of the UK *Highway Code*

- **Safety equipment** – Children under the age of 14 must wear a helmet which complies with the most up-to-date regulations. It must be fastened securely. It is strongly advised that all other riders follow these requirements also. These requirements do not apply to a child who is a follower of the Sikh religion and wearing a turban.

- **Help yourself be seen!**

  You should wear:

  ❏ Boots or shoes with hard soles and heels.

  ❏ Light-coloured or fluorescent clothing in daylight.

  ❏ Reflective clothing if you have to ride at night or in poor visibility.

Please note the BHS do not recommend night time riding.

- **Riding at night** – It is safer not to ride at night or in poor visibility but if you must, make sure you wear reflective clothing and your horse has reflective bands above the fetlock joints. A light that shows white to the front and red to the rear should be fitted, with a band, to the rider's right arm and/or leg/riding boot. If you are leading a horse at night on foot, carry a light in your right hand, showing white to the front and red to the rear and ensure both horse and rider are wearing reflective kit. It is strongly recommended that this includes a fluorescent/reflective tail guard for the horse.

- **Before riding** – You should:

  ❑ Ensure all tack fits well and is in good condition.

  ❑ Make sure you can control the horse. Always ride with other, less nervous, horses if you think that your horse will be nervous of traffic. Never ride a horse without both a saddle and a bridle.

- **Before riding off** – Always look behind you to make sure it is safe, and then give a clear arm signal. When riding on the road you should:

  ❑ Keep to the left.

  ❑ Keep both hands on the reins unless you are signalling.

  ❑ Keep both feet in the stirrups.

  ❑ Not carry another person.

  ❑ Not carry anything that might affect your balance or get tangled up with your reins.

  ❑ Keep a horse you are leading to your left.

  ❑ Move in the direction of the traffic flow in a one-way street.

  ❑ Never ride more than two abreast, and ride in single file on narrow or busy roads and when riding round bends.

- **Footpaths*, pavements and cycle tracks** – You must not take a horse on to a footpath or pavement, although you may be able to take a horse on to a cycle track. Use a bridleway/equestrian route where possible. Equestrian crossings may be provided for horse riders to cross the road and you should use these where available. You should dismount at a level crossing where a 'Horse Rider Dismount' sign is displayed. **Note exceptions**, you may be able to ride on a footpath with permission of the landowner. Some cycle tracks do not preclude use by horse riders.

*Footpath in this context refers to a footway alongside roads – see Highways Code Act 1835.

- **Roundabouts** – Avoid roundabouts wherever possible. If you use them you should:

  ❏ Keep to the left and watch out for vehicles crossing your path to leave or join the roundabout.

  ❏ Signal right when riding across exits to show you are not leaving.

  ❏ Signal left just before you leave the roundabout.

Dead Slow campaign

We launched the Dead Slow campaign in 2016 to encourage drivers to slow down and be aware of how they should drive safely around horses and riders on the road. Dead Slow aims to make drivers aware of the need to slow down to a maximum of 15mph when they encounter a horse and rider on the road and allow at least a car's width between the car and the horse.

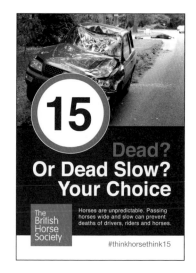

We would encourage all riders to familiarise themselves with the UK *Highway Code* rules below, which are aimed at drivers. Some of the information below is also relevant to horse riders as it outlines how you should behave and interact with other traffic whilst on the road.

We have four simple steps for drivers. If I see a horse on a road then I will:

1. Slow down to a maximum of 15mph.

2. Be patient, I won't sound my horn or rev my engine.

3. Pass the horse wide and slow (if safe to do so) at least a car's width if possible.

4. Drive slowly away.

Driver-specific sections of the UK *Highway Code*

*   **Animals** – When passing animals, drive slowly. Give them plenty of room and be ready to stop. Do not scare animals by sounding your horn, revving your engine or accelerating rapidly once you have passed them. Look out for animals being led, driven or ridden on the road and take extra care. Keep your speed down at bends and on narrow country roads. If a road is blocked by a herd of animals, stop and switch off your engine until they have left the road. Watch out for animals on unfenced roads.

- **Horse riders and horse-drawn vehicles** – Be particularly careful of horse riders and horse-drawn vehicles especially when overtaking. Always pass wide and slowly. Horse riders are often children, so take extra care and remember riders may ride in double file when escorting a young or inexperienced horse or rider. Look out for horse riders' and horse drivers' signals and heed a request to slow down or stop. Take great care and treat all horses as a potential hazard; they can be unpredictable, despite the efforts of their rider/driver.

- Take extra care at junctions. You should:

  ❏ Watch out for cyclists, motorcyclists, powered wheelchairs/mobility scooters and pedestrians as they are not always easy to see. Be aware that they may not have seen or heard you if you are approaching from behind.

  ❏ Watch out for pedestrians crossing a road into which you are turning. If they have started to cross they have priority, so give way.

  ❏ Watch out for long vehicles that may be turning at a junction ahead; they may have to use the whole width of the road to make the turn.

  ❏ Watch out for horse riders who may take a different line on the road from that which you would expect.

  ❏ Not assume, when waiting at a junction, that a vehicle coming from the right and signalling left will actually turn. Wait and make sure.

  ❏ Look all around before emerging. Do not cross or join a road until there is a gap large enough for you to do so safely.

- You must stop behind the line at a junction with a 'Stop' sign and a solid white line across the road. Wait for a safe gap in the traffic before you move off.

- The approach to a junction may have a 'Give Way' sign or a triangle marked on the road. You must give way to traffic on the main road when emerging from a junction with broken white lines across the road.

- Signals warn and inform other road users, including pedestrians, of your intended actions. You should always:

  ❏ Give clear signals in plenty of time, having checked it is not misleading to signal at that time.

  ❏ Use them to advise other road users before changing course or direction, stopping or moving off.

  ❏ Cancel them after use.

  ❏ Make sure your signals will not confuse others. If, for instance, you want to stop after a side road, do not signal until you are passing the road. If you signal earlier it may give the impression that you intend to turn into the road. Your brake lights will warn traffic behind you that you are slowing down.

  ❏ Use an arm signal to emphasise or reinforce your signal if necessary. Remember that signalling does not give you priority.

- You should also:

  ❏ Watch out for signals given by other road users and proceed only when you are satisfied that it is safe.

  ❏ Be aware that an indicator on another vehicle may not have been cancelled.

- You must obey signals given by police officers, traffic officers, traffic wardens and signs used by school crossing patrols.

- Never assume that flashing headlights is a signal inviting you to proceed. Use your own judgement and proceed carefully.

- **Safe driving or riding needs concentration** – Avoid distractions such as:

  ❏ Loud music (this may mask other sounds).

  ❏ Trying to read maps.

- ❏ Starting or adjusting any music or radio.

- ❏ Arguing with other road users.

- ❏ Eating and drinking.

- ❏ Smoking.

- **Before overtaking** you should make sure:

  - ❏ The road is sufficiently clear ahead.

  - ❏ Road users are not beginning to overtake you.

  - ❏ There is a suitable gap in front of the road user you plan to overtake.

- **Overtake only** when it is safe and legal to do so. You should:

  - ❏ Not get too close to the vehicle you intend to overtake.

  - ❏ Signal when it is safe to do so, take a quick sideways glance if necessary into the blind spot area and then start to move out.

  - ❏ Not assume that you can simply follow a vehicle ahead that is overtaking; there may be only enough room for one vehicle.

  - ❏ Allow plenty of room. Move back to the left as soon as you can, but do not cut in.

  - ❏ Take extra care at night and in poor visibility when it is harder to judge speed and distance.

  - ❏ Give way to oncoming vehicles before passing parked vehicles or other obstructions on your side of the road. Only overtake on the left if the vehicle in front is signalling to turn right and it is safe to do so.

  - ❏ Stay in your lane if traffic is moving slowly in queues. If the queue on your right is moving more slowly than you are, you may pass on the left.

- ❏ Give motorcyclists, cyclists and horse riders at least as much room as you would when overtaking a car.

- You must stop behind the white 'Stop' line across your side of the road unless the light is green. If the amber light appears you may go on only if you have already crossed the stop line or are so close to it that to stop might cause a collision.

- You must not move forward over the white line when the red light is showing. Only go forward when the traffic lights are green if there is room for you to clear the junction safely or you are taking up a position to turn right. If the traffic lights are not working, treat the situation as you would an unmarked junction and proceed with great care.

- Wait until there is a safe gap between you and any oncoming vehicle. Watch out for cyclists, motorcyclists, pedestrians and other road users. Check the blind spot again to make sure you are not being overtaken, and then make the turn. Do not cut the corner. Take great care when turning into a main road; you will need to watch for traffic in both directions and wait for a safe gap.

- Give a left-turn signal well before you turn left. Do not overtake just before you turn left and watch out for traffic coming up on your left before you make the turn. Cyclists, motorcyclists and other road users in particular may be hidden from your view.

- At roundabouts, watch out for and give plenty of room to:

  - ❏ Pedestrians who may be crossing the approach and exit roads.

  - ❏ Traffic crossing in front of you on the roundabout, especially vehicles intending to leave by the next exit.

  - ❏ Traffic that may be straddling lanes or positioned incorrectly.

  - ❏ Motorcyclists.

  - ❏ Cyclists and horse riders who may stay in the left-hand lane and signal right if they intend to continue round the roundabout. Allow them to do so.

❏ Long vehicles (including those towing trailers). These might have to take a different course or straddle lanes either approaching or on the roundabout because of their length. Watch out for their signals.

Road markings and what they mean

● Give way to traffic on major road

= = = = = = = = = = = = =

● Give way to traffic from the right at a roundabout

─ ── ── ── ── ── ── ── ── ── ── ── ─

● Give way to traffic from the right at a mini-roundabout

─ ─ ─ ─ ─ ─ ─ ─ ─ ─ ─ ─ ─ ─ ─ ─ ─ ─ ─

● Stop line at signals or police control

─────────────────────────

Road signs and shapes

The shape and colour of a road sign can change its meaning. It is important that as a horse rider you are aware of some of the most common road signs and what they could mean for you. For example, circular signs give orders to road users, such as stop and no entry, and triangular signs warn of things such as slippery roads or a crossroad.

Common road signs to be aware of:

Roadworks	School	Low-flying aircraft	Bend to right
Cattle	Crossroads	Double bend	Level crossing with barrier
Level crossing without barrier	Roundabout	Slippery road	Wild horses
Give way	Give way to oncoming traffic	Stop	
No left turn	National speed limit	No right turn	

For more information regarding all road signs please look at your regional *Highway Code*.

For the Republic of Ireland please refer to the *Rules of the Road*.

Stop

Loose chippings

Accompanied
horses & ponies

Yield

National speed limit

Mini roundabout ahead

Y-junction

50km/h speed limit

Keep straight ahead

No ridden or
accompanied horses

Cattle or Farm
Animals

Detour to right

Traffic signals ahead

No entry

Unguarded level
crossing ahead

Advance sign for lay-by
with tourist attraction

Summary

- Within the *Highway Code* there are lots of rules that all road users need to abide by.

- Some rules are specific for horse riders so you should be aware of these before riding out on the road.

- The UK and Republic of Ireland share a lot of road signs but it is important to know the difference and what signs relate to you in your location.

- We have launched a Dead Slow campaign to try and educate other road users on how to pass horse riders out on the road.

TRAINING TIPS

1. Read over the rules within the *Highway Code* that relates directly to horse riders so you are familiar with them.

2. Have a look at road signs when you are out and about and look up what the road sign means and how traffic might act on the road and how this may impact you whilst riding on the road.

3. Read other rules relating to car drivers so you are familiar with car users rules.

4. Together with a group of friends, train each other on road signs.